M000287127

THE CONCISE
APA HANDBOOK

THE CONCISE
APA HANDBOOK

By Paul Chamness Miller
Rachael Ruegg
Naoko Araki
Mary Frances Agnello
Mark de Boer
Akita International University

Information Age Publishing, Inc.
Charlotte, North Carolina • www.infoagepub.com

Library of Congress Cataloging-in-Publication Data

CIP data for this book can be found on the Library of Congress website:
http://www.loc.gov/index.html

Paperback: 978-1-68123-773-2
Hardcover: 978-1-68123-774-9
E-Book: 978-1-68123-775-6

Copyright © 2017 IAP–Information Age Publishing, Inc.

All rights reserved. No part of this publication may be reproduced, stored in a retrieval system, or transmitted in any form or by any electronic or mechanical means, or by photocopying, microfilming, recording or otherwise without written permission from the publisher.

Printed in the United States of America.

CONTENTS

PREFACE

We, the authors of *The Concise APA Handbook*, are all experienced teachers of writing, especially in teaching students whose first language is not English. We have never found the ideal book to help our students understand how to format their paper according to the format that is prescribed by our university, the guidelines spelled out by the American Psychological Association (APA). Consequently, we came together and pooled our many years of experience as teachers of English learners, writing and research courses, and mentors of graduate students to write this handbook, with the hope that it will be a user-friendly, concise resource that gives students the "nuts and bolts" of writing academic papers with easy-to-understand language.

The topics we chose to address are all issues that we have found to be common concerns in helping our own students learn how to use references appropriately and format their papers according to specific requirements. As you will see, we have provided the basic ideas behind why using references is necessary, understanding avoiding plagiarism, finding and evaluating sources, citing sources in the text, creating a reference list, and formatting your paper according to APA guidelines. Where appropriate, we have included a variety of images and examples to help illustrate the points being made.

As this is a concise APA handbook, we have only included the most important points and most common examples in writing an academic paper, based on our own personal experiences. For more in-depth information about APA, you should refer to the *Publication Manual of the American Psychological Association* (http://www.apastyle.org/manual/index.aspx), which you may find in your local library or easily purchased through your favorite bookstore. There are also several very useful websites that provide more details and examples for citing less commonly used sources. Two of

The Concise APA Handbook
pp. vii–viii
Copyright © 2017 by Information Age Publishing
All rights of reproduction in any form reserved.

the most common are OWL, Purdue University's Online Writing Lab APA website (https://owl.english.purdue.edu/owl/resource/560/1/) and the APA Style Blog, which is sponsored by APA (http://blog.apastyle.org).

ACKNOWLEDGMENT

We would like to give a special thank you to Mr. Juan Francisco de Haro Ruiz for his wonderful cover design. Anyone interested in his work as a graphic artist can reach him by e-mail at juanfranciscodeharo@gmail.com.

1

WHAT IS REFERENCING AND WHY DO WE NEED IT?

When we join the academic community as students, we adopt the language and expectations of behavior in a learning and researching community. When we are learning how to write formal papers in university writing classes, we rely on some traditions of studying rhetoric and how to write original papers. Much of what we discuss or write about in the academic or literary community is shared information. As we become more experienced students, we learn how to use the ideas of others without claiming them as our own. Such an activity is the accepted way of relying on others' ideas to support and enhance our own. The way to reference or cite others' text is called referencing. When we rely on a specific author or his or her ideas, we write a citation to give credit to the person who published or wrote the idea originally. Referencing, in general, serves a dual purpose—first, to acknowledge within the actual body of the students' writing the source of information, and second, to provide at the end of the text a more detailed alphabetical listing of the students' cited references.

Referencing, according to *Webster's New World College Dictionary*, is referring to a greater authority than ourselves on certain topics and bodies of information when we are writing about or using ideas that are not our own or that we have found in some reputable resource, especially when we are doing research (Agnes & Guralnik, 2010, p. 1203). The reasons that we reference in our writing include the following:

The Concise APA Handbook
pp. 1–3
Copyright © 2017 by Information Age Publishing
All rights of reproduction in any form reserved.

1

- to show sincerity,
- to demonstrate ethical behavior, and
- to reveal that we have joined the academic community's communication system on which we rely to provide us with the information about similar work that others have done in the past.

Referencing shows sincerity by revealing that we have relied on others' work to help us do our own. Referencing demonstrates ethical behavior because in doing so we are acting in an ethical or correct way, which is to share with others the sources from which we derived assistance with our work. We act in such a manner because those who made the research available to us deserve some acknowledgment. By referencing others' knowledge, we also exhibit our mastery of one of the academic community's discourses or languages of intercommunication. We show through the conventions of citing our sources of knowledge or information that we understand how the academic community functions by acknowledging others' expertise in many subject areas.

Relying on the research and writing of other experts is what the researcher does routinely. As students become researchers, they are working within the realm of information gathering. The research papers usually assigned in advanced levels of language learning are long reports with a specific rhetorical goal—usually to cover some body of information, to define a concept, or perhaps to combine many resources that reveal academic work or significant areas of investigation and findings. Referencing is done according to different rules and guidelines.

All institutions and the many disciplines within them have their own research traditions and citation systems. The biggest difference in all of the reference systems is style; otherwise all of them focus on similar components: authors, titles or names of articles, books or websites, dates and places of publication, and names of publishers. Your institution relies on its own reference system, and you should try to master what is needed in order to use it wisely and well. In essence, we get out of the effort to do good referencing in our writing what we put into it.

There is an expression in the computer world that says "garbage in and garbage out." We do not wish for our learning and the projects that take many of our efforts in the learning process to be inferior. Therefore, we must take pride in the citing and referencing act. We must also appreciate the problems that can result from not taking pride in our work done through the vehicles of speaking, reading, and writing. When we rely on others' knowledge and information to accomplish our tasks, we must make available various kinds of information regarding the sources of our information to illustrate the effort we have made.

This chapter terminates with a reference section so that you will see the proper way to cite the work(s) consulted in order to compose our original text. You will learn by seeing examples of how to do referencing and citing throughout this book. You will also exercise your new learning about referencing and citations by persevering and understanding the specific ways in which to cite the kind of resources that you are using. We must all remember that citations and references take effort on your part as a learner, a writer, a researcher, and a citizen of the academic community. Like in most of our learning and mastery of the kinds of skills that we wish to learn in life, we derive the greatest results when we work hard at something.

Enjoy your APA journey. It is one that will keep you on the proper path of learning and that is actually fun to implement in your writing, because it is a challenge that the best of all academic community participants understands and relies on routinely.

REFERENCE

Agnes, M., & Guralnik, D. B. (Eds.). (2010). *Webster's new world college dictionary* (4th ed.). Cleveland, OH: Wiley.

2

PLAGIARISM

Plagiarism is a form of passing off something that is not ours as our own. Simply put, it is a form of stealing. In the world of academic work, ideas are abstractions. Taking someone's ideas can be difficult to prove sometimes; however, there are many ways that an experienced teacher or researcher can discern if someone has plagiarized or taken others' work in an unethical manner. One instance of plagiarism can be accomplished by paying another person to write an essay or to do an assignment. An archetypal example of plagiarism is doing a Google search on a chosen essay topic and finding a readymade essay online which can be submitted to the teacher with minor changes such as reformatting, or taking an essay written by another student and submitting it as one's own. However, these examples are far from a complete illustration of plagiarism. In reality, like many aspects of writing, plagiarism is a very complex and subjective issue, with few simple black and white answers. Many students may think that if they did not plagiarize on purpose, they are innocent of plagiarism. In reality, the majority of cases of plagiarism are accidental. People commit plagiarism because they do not realize that what they are doing is a form of plagiarism, because they are not careful when using in-text citation and referencing, or even because of weak language skills. The purpose of this chapter is to deepen the reader's understanding of the issue of plagiarism, of what constitutes plagiarism, and of writing practices to avoid. The reasons that we learn what plagiarism is and how not to plagiarize are to avoid being accused of plagiarism and to benefit as much as possible from the learning process.

The Concise APA Handbook
pp. 5–12
Copyright © 2017 by Information Age Publishing
All rights of reproduction in any form reserved.

TWO BASIC RULES TO FOLLOW TO AVOID PLAGIARISM

At the most basic level, there are two rules which need to be followed in order to avoid committing plagiarism. Many people believe that to prevent plagiarism they should write their own ideas and, if any of their ideas do come from another source, they should acknowledge the source where the ideas came from, using an in-text citation and a reference. This is true, but writing one's own ideas and acknowledging the ideas of others is only one of the two basic rules.

Another important basic rule is for students to use their own words in their writing. There are many cases in which a writer may have thought of original and unique ideas, but still plagiarize by not writing the ideas in their own words. Some examples of plagiarism of language include the following:

- using translation software, without clearly indicating which part of the text was translated and which software was used for the translation work (of course using a dictionary to translate individual words or phrases is perfectly fine, indeed learners with additional languages should do so),
- patch writing, and
- having your writing corrected by someone who is better at writing.

A MORE DETAILED EXAMINATION OF AVOIDING PLAGIARISM

According to Williams and Carroll (2009), the following activities are forms of plagiarism:

- someone else searching for and choosing materials for you to use in your writing,
- using someone else's notes as the basis for your writing,
- talking to others and copying the ideas they say into your writing, and
- getting help with proofreading/checking or editing, if the writing is for a language or writing class, which entails evaluating the quality of the writing.

Having someone else search for and choose materials for you falls under the first rule. Searching for and selecting appropriate materials for your writing is a part of the writer's job. If someone has chosen which materials you will focus on in your writing, then they have influenced what you will say about the topic in an important way. For example, imagine you are writing an argument essay about the death penalty and the person has chosen only materials that argue against the death penalty. This will limit your ability to understand the topic fully and may also influence what you include in your essay as the main points. One exception to the idea of searching for and selecting your own materials is when the teacher who sets the assignment asks you to focus on specific readings. They may do this in a writing class as a way of making the process easier for you (not having to search for and find materials means one less thing you need to worry about) or because they are teaching about in-text citation and referencing (if you are referring to a material that teachers are familiar with, it will be easier for them to see how well you have understood and how appropriately you have used the information in your writing). In a content class, teachers may do this because having a solid understanding of those particular readings is important in order to understand the topic. More often than not, even when you are asked to refer to particular readings by your teacher, your teacher would be pleased to see that you had read and included additional materials about the topic in your writing.

Using someone else's notes is more problematic than someone else choosing the materials for you to read because there is the possibility that the person misunderstood the reading or lecture and this wrong information will be included in your essay. Some notes may also be the note taker's original opinion about the topic rather than having come directly from another source. Talking to others about the topic and then copying their ideas into your writing is closer to the archetypal definition of plagiarism in that it is taking someone else's ideas and representing them as your own. Ideas gleaned from others through conversations can be used in order to gain a broader understanding of other people's opinions about the topic. However, one person's opinion should not be conveyed in writing exactly as they have explained it. Rather it should be a point of interest that leads the writer to do further research on a particular aspect of the topic, through which they can form their own opinion and formulate it in their own words.

Getting help from others constitutes plagiarism if what the person does could be described as "correcting" or "editing" your writing. However, this is usually only the case when your writing will be assessed for its quality, such as in a language or writing skills class. In a language or writing skills class, the teacher needs to evaluate your writing skills (which includes aspects such as tone, writing style, and appropriate register) and/or the grammatical and lexical accuracy of your writing. If someone else has edited your writing, then the teacher cannot see writing which has been written by you, which would enable them to evaluate your skills. On the other hand, this does not mean that you should not ask other writers for help. Indeed, asking other writers for help is one of the best ways to improve your writing skills. When you ask for help from other writers, they should offer you advice or explain points to you (such as grammatical rules). If they pick up a pen (or use the keyboard) to write on your draft then there is a strong chance that what they are doing is correcting, rather than offering advice (i.e., writing for you, rather than helping you to write). The difference between doing the first action and the second is not always obvious, yet we need to be careful about the ways that we seek help with our writing and also about the manner in which we offer our assistance to others. However, basically helping you would entail explaining aspects of grammar or writing style to you and plagiarism would entail providing you with suitable expressions, phrases, or sentences that can be inserted directly into your text. Quantity also plays a part in distinguishing help from plagiarism. If another writer suggests one word, which can be used to convey the meaning you are trying to convey, then it is much like using a dictionary and is clearly not problematic. On the other hand, if the writing adviser or helper goes through your draft and offers a number of words that would be better alternatives to the ones in the current draft, then the help reaches a point where it could be said that not all of the language in the revised version of the essay is your own. Especially if you are writing in an additional language, be careful not to let others help you too much with the language in your writing.

From these points made by Williams and Carroll (2009), we can see that writers need to have done all aspects of the writing process themselves in order to truly avoid plagiarism: finding source materials, selecting appropriate ones, making notes, writing the draft, revising the draft, and proofreading the final draft before submission. There is another kind of plagiarism not included in the list above—self-plagiarism.

SELF-PLAGIARISM

Many students are surprised to hear about the concept of self-plagiarism and have an entrenched belief that as long as the ideas and words in an assignment are their own then they cannot be accused of plagiarism. It is true that self-plagiarism applies mainly to academics, professors, or researchers who publish their writing in a magazine or journal and then resubmit the same content for publication in another journal or magazine. This is because a journal or magazine article is supposed to be an original contribution to the field of study. If the article has already been published, then it is clearly not original.

Similarly, though, what students submit for an assignment is supposed to be their own original work. Therefore, if a student submits the same essay to two different teachers for two different courses, the student has committed self-plagiarism. Essentially the student is getting double credit for the work. Although clearly using the same topic and some of the same ideas for multiple assignments is fairly common, there is a point at which even two different essays can exemplify self-plagiarism.

Once again, the boundary between acceptable reuse of ideas and self-plagiarism comes down to quantity. Each writer tends to have their own writing style and their wording is likely to be similar, even when they are writing about completely different topics. On the other hand, if a chunk of writing is exactly the same, word for word, as what the student wrote in another essay, then they have committed self-plagiarism. A sentence or two is acceptable, but several sentences crosses the boundary. Similarly, if a student writes two essays in two different classes in which exactly the same main points are used, even if one essay has been paraphrased into different words, this constitutes self-plagiarism. On the other hand, it would usually be considered acceptable for one or two of the main points from one essay to be reused in another essay as long as they are expressed differently (provided the essay has a number of other main points).

PATCH WRITING

The act of taking the writing of others and maintaining the sentence structure, while substituting the original words with others is called patch writing, and is another form of plagiarism. Patch writing does not include the ideas of the original author, and therefore is different from paraphrasing. Rather, only the sentence structure is incorporated into another text. See the following example:

Original text:

In order to find out whether religion had any effect on people's attitudes toward sex before marriage, a questionnaire which asked about participants' religious affiliation as well as their attitudes toward sex before marriage, was disseminated and analyzed. The results indicated that religious affiliation had no effect on attitudes toward sex before marriage.

Patch written text:

In order to find out whether income had any effect on people's drinking habits, a questionnaire which asked about participants' income as well as their drinking habits, was disseminated and analyzed. The results indicated that income had a significant effect on drinking habits.

Flowerdew and Li (2007) found that many students believe that "as long as the work is their own, the language can be borrowed ... from one text into another" (pp. 459–460). However, as explained above, avoiding plagiarism means both writing one's own ideas and using one's own language. Therefore, this belief Flowerdew and Li's students had (and that probably many other students around the world have) is incorrect.

LANGUAGE PROFICIENCY-RELATED PLAGIARISM

In addition to all the different kinds of plagiarism mentioned so far, for students who are learning in an additional language, there are other kinds of plagiarism which are caused by weak language skills. In order to avoid plagiarism, not only should the ideas and the words be the writers' own, but also any ideas or words that do come from another source, such as a book, journal, or website, should be either quoted or paraphrased, with a corresponding in-text citation and reference.

Moreover, it is important that paraphrased information correctly conveys what the original author intended. It is not enough to simply maintain the original sentence structure and replace words with synonyms, rather the sentence structure should also be changed so that the language is the writer's own, although the idea has come from another source. This poses a number of problems for students who are learning in an additional language. First, it is important that source materials which are read by the writer are fully understood. At least, any ideas which the writer would like to use in their essay need to be understood fully in order to be successfully paraphrased into the writer's own words. Also, the writer needs a relatively broad knowledge of grammar and vocabulary in order to ensure that the paraphrased sentence they write actually does mean what they intend it to. It is the writer's responsibility to make sure that what they write in a paraphrase has the same meaning as that which was conveyed in the source material. If the paraphrase misrepresents what the original author wrote, due to a lack of complete understanding, or a lack of grammatical or vocabulary knowledge, that misrepresentation is another kind of plagiarism. Although writers might not intentionally plagiarize, if they commit plagiarism, even unintentionally, there will often be very serious consequences. The following section will explain some of the possible consequences of plagiarism, giving specific examples of past cases of plagiarism.

THE CONSEQUENCES OF PLAGIARISM

We might be surprised at how painful and harsh the consequences of plagiarism can be. The ways in which plagiarism is dealt with vary from place to place. Informing ourselves about what plagiarism is, as well as our local school or university's consequences for plagiarism, is something that we can all do by looking in the institution's policy handbook. The simplest punishment for plagiarism has implications for one's career and livelihood, and in some cases for one's professional career and life. Because plagiarism usually means the revoking of academic credentials, the professional position of a person working in the university can be taken away in punishment by an institution. When plagiarism was committed intentionally, many people punish themselves by feeling shame and guilt and in the most extreme cases this can lead to suicide. In the case of student plagiarism, the most common punishment applied by universities around the world for plagiarism is to expel the student from the university, just as they do for committing other unethical behavior such as cheating on assignments, exams, or projects. Even if the punishment is not so severe, it can cause hardships. For example, sometimes a university will deny all course credits during the semester in which the offense was committed to students who are guilty. Such a punishment may translate into wasted time, money, and study efforts, in addition to a setback in academic and work projections.

If we look beneath the surface of the obvious turmoil that verified cases of plagiarism can cause, we can understand that the act of plagiarism usually involved a theft—a stealing of ideas, of words, of theories, of research findings, or some other falsification that essentially means that a writer or researcher has claimed ownership or discoveries that are false. As for the student who is accused of plagiarism, he or she has used words or ideas that were not original and claimed them unethically in writing compositions or research projects.

In the case of professors or high-ranking administrators in universities losing their posts in a university system, we must understand such individuals are supposed to model exemplary behavior and ethics for all of the people in the institution from the teachers and researchers, to the staff, and students. Because unethical behavior results from the bad decision to make false claims about one's work, the plagiarist who has attained a high-ranking position has done so under false pretenses. Thus, the example set for all of the other professionals, staff, and students who are often paying for their education is not a good one. In fact, the plagiarist is the opposite of the kind of person who would set the behavioral or ethical standard for others to follow in an educational system. However, even when plagiarism is committed unintentionally, revoking the academic credential and the corresponding demotion or termination of employment is still considered justified as the plagiarism makes it unclear whether the person has attained the level of expertise that would have been required to have gained that qualification without plagiarizing. Thus, we should all remember that even if a plagiarist used others' work unintentionally, the consequences are harsh nonetheless.

A FINAL WORD ABOUT PLAGIARISM

As can be seen throughout the discussion of plagiarism, plagiarism is difficult to avoid. It is especially difficult for students who are struggling with a large amount of reading and writing in an additional language. Yet the consequences of plagiarism can also be severe. With an increased understanding of plagiarism, you might feel that it will be incredibly difficult to avoid and be unsure how to proceed.

As a general rule, a writing tutor would be a good place to turn. If there are no writing tutors available to you, then turn to your teacher for help. Explain to them what kinds of troubles you have and what you need help with. Most importantly, if you have completed an assignment and feel like you might have unintentionally plagiarized, it is important to discuss this with the tutor or teacher **before** you submit the writing. Once the writing has been submitted, any procedures which the school or learning institution implements in cases of plagiarism can be applied. On the other hand, if you have not yet submitted the writing, no consequences will usually be applied and you will have a chance to resolve the problem before submitting the assignment, as long as time permits. Indeed, the sooner you discuss any problems you have, the earlier you will be able to receive help to avoid plagiarism and the more effective that help will be.

REFERENCES

Flowerdew, J., & Li, Y. (2007). Language re-use among Chinese apprentice scientists writing for publication. *Applied Linguistics, 28,* 440–465. doi:10.1093/applin/amm031

Williams, K., & Carroll, J. (2009). *Referencing and understanding plagiarism.* London, England: Palgrave Macmillan.

3

EVALUATING SOURCES FOR ACADEMIC WORK

When you look for general information online, you will probably use Google to search for specific information. Google is a useful site to find any general information. It gives you news, visual images including videos, but when searching for *academic* standard materials, these (.com) sites are not so reliable.

If you google the words "World Heritage," the site shows 85,500,000 results (see Figure 3.1). This includes personal opinions of World Heritage. These days, anyone can create a website and upload any information online. Of course, you can also find international organization (.org) or government sites (.gov) by using Google.

Another popular site that students tend to use is Wikipedia, a free encyclopedia. It is available in a range of languages, but it is not a reliable site for writing an academic paper. Wikipedia is created based on a belief that everyone should have access to knowledge for free; therefore, the site has an Edit button on the right hand corner to allow users to add, omit, and change any information on the site. Even if a person is not an expert on World Heritage sites, she or he can easily manipulate the information on Wikipedia. In this sense, it is not a reliable site.

For academic sources, there are useful and academically specific sites that students can go to. One of the sites is called Google Scholar (https://scholar.google.com). You can find academic books, e-books, journals, online journals, theses, and reports in various academic fields. See Figures

The Concise APA Handbook
pp. 13–25
Copyright © 2017 by Information Age Publishing
All rights of reproduction in any form reserved.

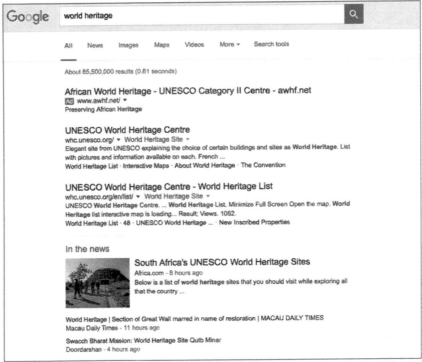

Google and the Google logo are registered trademarks of Google Inc., used with permission.

Figure 3.1. Example of a basic Google search.

3.2 and 3.3 for a comparison of the main Google and Google Scholar pages.

Google and the Google logo are registered trademarks of Google Inc., used with permission.

Figure 3.2. Google.

Google and the Google logo are registered trademarks of Google Inc., used with permission.

Figure 3.3. Google Scholar.

Using the same key words, "World Heritage," in Google Scholar, it shows 2,380,000 results. If you compare that reduced number of results to the greater number found in Google's general search, the dramatic difference suggests most of the materials found in a general Google search are nonscholarly work.

DETAILS ABOUT HOW TO ACCESS GOOGLE SCHOLAR

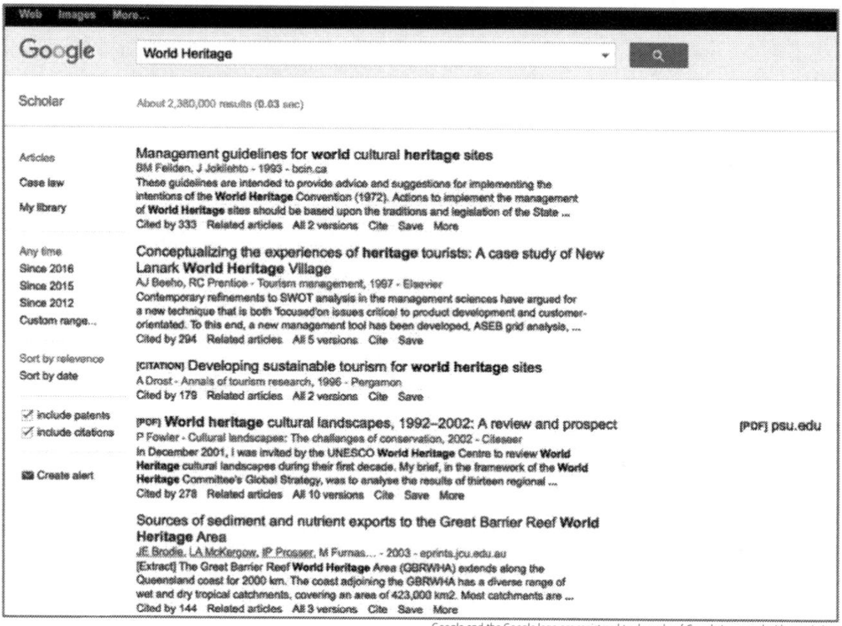

Google and the Google logo are registered trademarks of Google Inc., used with permission.

Figure 3.4.   Sample Google Scholar search.

The results of a search in Google Scholar include books, e-books, and journals in academic fields. A source followed by [PDF] means students can download the source in a full-text version. It is best to click the ones that you are interested in, and read an abstract or summary of the source before purchasing or downloading the material.

BROADENING AND NARROWING THE SEARCH

On Google Scholar, you can broaden or narrow the search using the general combine connectors. Common combine connectors for searching sources are AND, OR, and NOT. Each term has a specific function in searching outside sources. "AND" gives you results which show both terms you typed. If you type "Education AND Literacy" (without quotes) the results suggest sources that cover **both** terms. "OR" offers a wider search and means you will receive results that have each term as well as both terms. For example, "Education OR Literacy" will suggest sources including Education only, Literacy only, as well as Education and Literacy sources. The last one, "NOT," specifies sources within particular keywords searches to leave out. "Education NOT Literacy," for example, means all sources on Education but excluding the ones with the keyword "Literacy." Figure 3.5 illustrates how these terms are used.

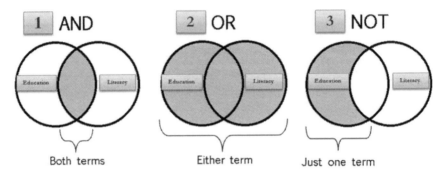

Figure 3.5. Example using combine connectors.

Let's have a look at how the terms are actually used in Google Scholar. The first term, "AND," is useful when students want to perform a combined search of both keywords, for example "World Heritage and Japan." In Google Scholar, the results show 636,000 hits and these results have two words "World Heritage" as well as "Japan" in the content (see Figure 3.6).

Another useful signal is the use of double quotation marks "...." This will help students to search an exact phrase search and will specify the search to a very narrow area. Putting the keywords, World Heritage Japan, in the double quotation marks, "World Heritage Japan," will give narrow search results of 21 academic sources on Google Scholar (see Figure 3.7).

With the use of double quotation marks, you can further narrow your search by combining the following signal abbreviations (Table 3.1).

Typing a combination of title (ti:) and keywords with double quotation marks ("bilingual education") will give limited results of six (see Figure 3.8).

It is often recommended to use recent academic materials for writing academic papers unless there are convincing reasons to use dated materi-

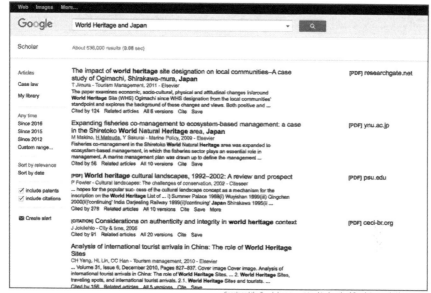

Google and the Google logo are registered trademarks of Google Inc., used with permission.

Figure 3.6.   Results in Google Scholar.

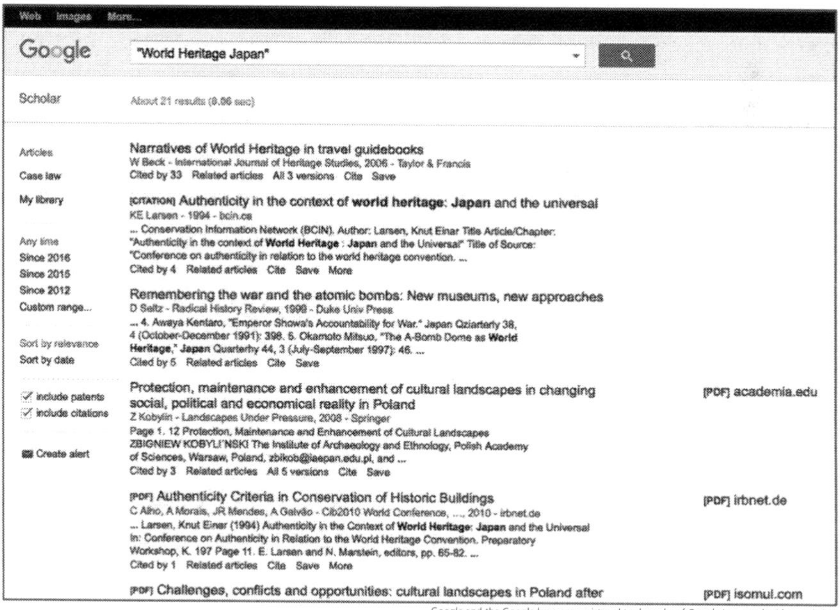

Google and the Google logo are registered trademarks of Google Inc., used with permission.

Figure 3.7.   Example of Google Scholar and quotations.

Table 3.1.	List of Signal Abbreviations
Abbreviation	**Returns Results From**
jo:	Names of journals
ti:	Titles
au:	Names of authors
ca:	Illustration captions
ty:fla	Full length articles
vo:	Volume of items
no:	Issue or number of items

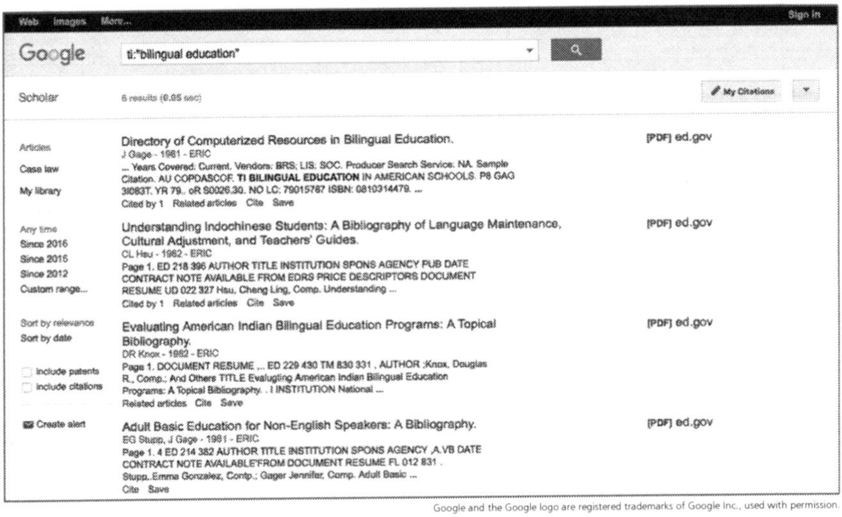

Google and the Google logo are registered trademarks of Google Inc., used with permission.

Figure 3.8.   Combination of quotations and signal abbreviation.

als (i.e., researching on Albert Einstein and focusing on his original books). When research results show a large number of academic materials, you can also narrow your search to recent publications. In Google Scholar, you can further limit the search by clicking a section on the left side of the page (e.g., since 2016, since 2015, and since 2012). You can also use the "custom range" function on the left and specify the year of publication (e.g., 2010–2016).

SEARCH ENGINES FOR ACADEMIC MATERIALS AT THE LIBRARY

Other online search engines are available through your university library. Each search engine has its strength. JSTOR, for example, contains journals, primary sources, and books, whereas LexisNexis provides full-text versions of news from newspapers and magazines throughout the world. Science Direct is another useful academic database.

JSTOR

Reprinted courtesy of JSTOR. JSTOR © 2016. All rights reserved.

Figure 3.9.   Homepage of JSTOR.

Clicking on "Advanced Search" at the center of the screen seen in Figure 3.9 will take you to the page seen in Figure 3.10.

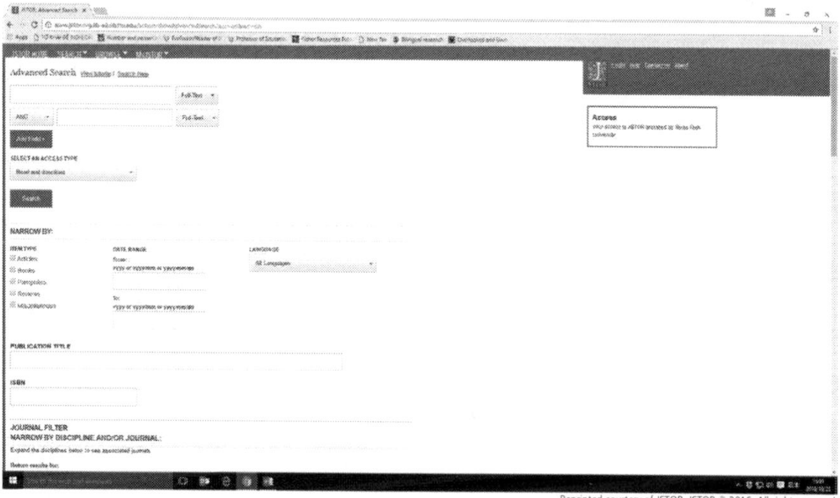

Reprinted courtesy of JSTOR. JSTOR © 2016. All rights reserved.

Figure 3.10.   Advanced search page of JSTOR.

It is recommended to search keywords with "Full-Text" in order to find sources in a full-text form (see Figure 3.11).

Reprinted courtesy of JSTOR. JSTOR © 2016. All rights reserved.

Figure 3.11. Searching for full-text sources.

For example, you type the following key words, "economics" AND "financial literacy." Using the advanced search, you can further narrow your search by types of sources (articles and books), publishing date, and language (see Figure 3.12).

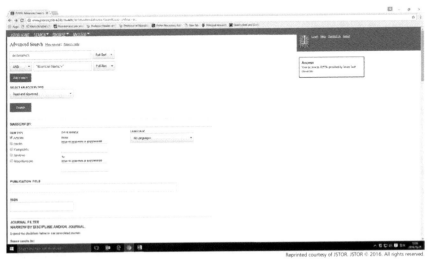

Reprinted courtesy of JSTOR. JSTOR © 2016. All rights reserved.

Figure 3.12. Example of advanced search.

The search result shows 272 sources with these key words (see Figure 3.13).

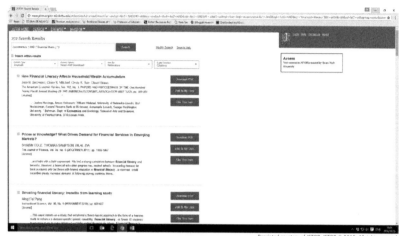

Reprinted courtesy of JSTOR. JSTOR © 2016. All rights reserved.

Figure 3.13.   Search results in JSTOR.

LexisNexis

Reprinted with the permission of LexisNexis.

Figure 3.14.   LexisNexis homepage for Japan and other countries.

LexisNexis has a range of functions for students to search for reliable sources (see Figure 3.14). Each section in Figure 3.15 shows a specific type of reference material you can get from the database. Note that Figures 3.14 and 3.15 are the current search interface for LexisNexis Academic in some countries like Japan. Figure 3.16 illustrates the current search interface for North America.

Reprinted with the permission of LexisNexis.

Figure 3.15. Description of LexisNexis search functions for the Japanese version.

Reprinted with the permission of LexisNexis.

Figure 3.16. LexisNexis homepage for North America.

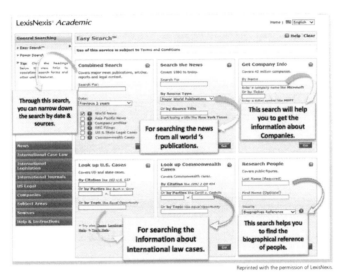

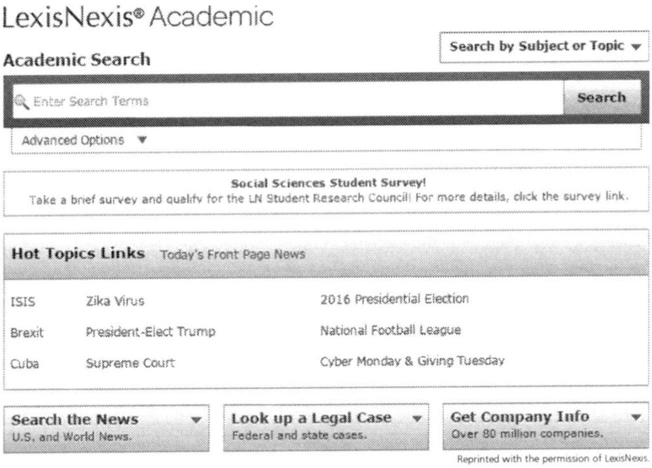

Once you type key words in LexisNexis, all the search results with different types of sources will appear on the screen as seen in Figure 3.17.

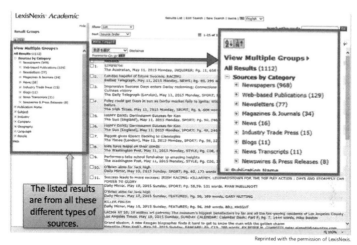

Figure 3.17. LexisNexis search results for all versions.

If you are specifically looking for a newspaper article, you simply click on "Newspapers" to see the results of the newspaper articles (see Figure 3.18).

Figure 3.18. LexisNexis newspaper results.

ScienceDirect

© 2016 by Elsevier. Used with permission.

Figure 3.19. ScienceDirect home page.

Typing the key words, construction engineering, for instance in ScienceDirect (Figure 3.19), it will show a list of relevant materials. Then, you can use the refine filters on the left side of the screen to narrow the search (see Figure 3.20).

© 2016 by Elsevier. Used with permission.

Figure 3.20. Example search results of ScienceDirect.

Each university has recommended search engines and databases for students. Some of these tools are designed for a specific discipline. Individual professors will have recommended search engines and databases, so it is best to ask them for suggestions in specific areas of study. Remember librarians are expert at locating sources and can help you with finding the academic materials you are looking for. They will also help with appropriate keywords if the search has not been so successful. When you need help in the library, do not hesitate to ask librarians for help. If you are searching online outside of the library, it is best to use the help functions on each search engine online or download the user manuals of the system.

FINDING RELEVANT SOURCES

Although the search engines are useful for finding academic sources, you still need to critically select sources from the search results. For example, if a source published in the 1980s appears on the first page of a search result with the key words "intercultural communication," blindly selecting the top five sources from the results is not recommended. Being listed on the first page does not mean that the sources are the most relevant ones you need for your assignment. You need to use your critical judgment when selecting appropriate sources. If a section of your assignment is on the history of "intercultural communication," a source published in the 1980s you found might be relevant to your assignment. However, if the focus of the assignment is on the current issues of "intercultural communication" and you are not discussing any history at all, a source published in the 1980s is not relevant as supporting evidence. Critical thinking skills are required for a selection of academic materials for your assignment. It is best to ask yourself the following question: How relevant is it to my assignment?

4

IN-TEXT CITATION

This chapter will explain how to cite a source material in one's writing. In-text citations are very important in order to avoid plagiarism and using them correctly is equally important. Incorrect use of in-text citations can lead to unintentional plagiarism.

There are two different ways of incorporating information taken from source materials into one's writing: quotation and paraphrasing. Regardless of whether text is quoted or paraphrased, both an in-text citation and a corresponding reference are needed. However, the information required in the in-text citation sometimes differs between quoted and paraphrased information.

QUOTATION AND PARAPHRASING

Quotation

Quotation is when words are taken from a source material and copied directly into one's writing. When a writer has done this, it is indicated by quotation marks around the copied words. Be careful not to use quotation too much in your writing because it can be difficult to follow writing that contains too many quotations. The following are some examples of quotation:

The Concise APA Handbook
pp. 27–37
Copyright © 2017 by Information Age Publishing
All rights of reproduction in any form reserved.

Original:

If learning style is influenced by one's sociocultural environment, it follows that teachers and students from similar backgrounds may have greater likelihood of similarity in ways of learning. Accordingly, teachers from minority backgrounds may be better prepared to meet the learning needs of an increasing proportion of the school population than teachers from other backgrounds.

Writing with in-text citation:

Zapata (1988) suggests that teachers who are of similar linguistic or racial groups as the students may serve as role models and "may be better prepared to meet the learning needs of an increasing proportion of the school population than teachers from other backgrounds" (p. 19).

Notice that the information for the entire sentence came from the source material. Therefore, the citation spans the entire sentence, with the name and year of publication of the original material at the beginning of the sentence and the page number from which the quotation was taken at the end of the sentence. Part of the information was written in the author's own words, so that part is not included in quotation marks. On the other hand, all of the words that appear exactly as they were in the original material are within the quotation marks. In this way, even though the information for the entire sentence came from the original material, the writer has demonstrated which information is written in their own words and which words are taken directly from the original material.

Original:

Inclusion of people of color must have at its core the recognition of the multiple ways in which we participate, see, and are in the world.

Writing with in-text citation:

Dillard (1994) argues, teacher education programs, administrators in school districts and others must recognize and acknowledge the richness that a diverse population of teachers brings, in the way they "participate, see, and are in the world" (p. 9), rather than merely focusing on numbers.

As in the previous example, this one includes both the writer's own words and words which were taken directly from the original text, except that the words taken directly from the original text are in the middle of the sentence rather than at the end. This example demonstrates the placement of the page number, directly after the quotation.

Alternatively, the author could have quoted all the information as follows:

Writing with in-text citation:

Dillard (1994) argues, "inclusion of people of color must have at its core the recognition of the multiple ways in which we participate, see and are in the world" (p. 9).

Let's look at another example:

Original:

Yamagata Prefectural Museum was established at Kajo Park in 1971. It is a general museum affiliated with the Yamagata Prefectural Education Museum and the Nature Study Garden.

There are many exhibits on natural history, history and culture in Yamagata Prefecture, including the *Jomon no Megami* (a goddess figure from the Jomon era, known as the Nishinomae ceramic figure), a nationally designated important cultural property, and *Daikaigyu* (Yamagata sea cow fossil), a prefectural natural monument.

Writing with in-text citation:

This museum houses Jomon-no-Megami, a *dogu* that has been designated a National Treasure of Japan and has received attention from experts throughout the world for its beautiful form and interesting stylization. A visitor to the museum's English webpage would have no idea how important this artifact is, as the only mention of the figure is on the homepage: "There are many exhibits on natural history, history and culture in Yamagata Prefecture, including the Jomon no Megami (a goddess figure from the Jomon era, known as the Nishinomae ceramic figure), a nationally designated important cultural property" (Yamagata Prefectural Museum, n.d., para. 2).

In this example, all of the information taken from the original material is quoted. The beginning of the sentence "A visitor to the museum's English webpage would have no idea how important this artifact is, as the only mention of the figure is on the homepage:" is the writer's original idea. In this case, since all the information from the original material is quoted, all components of the in-text citation appear together at the end of the sentence. Notice that instead of an author's name, this in-text citation has the name of an organization. This is done when the author's name is not provided in the original material, but the organization is clearly indicated as the author of the material. Notice also the use of "n.d." instead of the date. This is done when the publication date is not provided in the original material. Finally, notice that the in-text citation gives a paragraph number ("para. 2") instead of a page number. This is done when the original material does not have page numbers.

Finally, if a quotation is more than 40 words in length, the formatting is different. In that case, instead of using quotation marks, the quotation is indented to set it apart from the rest of the text. Note also that the punctuation goes after the sentence, rather than after the citation. See the following example:

Original:

Learner autonomy is a complex system, in which psychological factors of an individual—the learner autonomy capacity, motivation, and agency—interact with elements of the sociocultural and political context, including peers, teachers, parents, policies, cultural norms and ideologies. Emerging from these interactions are varying degrees of self-direction over learning, a high degree of which enable individuals to pursue personally meaningful goals and make in impact on their social context.

Writing with quotation:

The most concise and comprehensive definition of learner autonomy is as follows:

> Learner autonomy is a complex system, in which psychological factors of an individual—the learner autonomy capacity, motivation, and agency—interact with elements of the sociocultural and political context, including peers, teachers, parents, policies, cultural norms and ideologies. Emerging from these interactions are varying degrees of self-direction over learning, a high degree of which enable individuals to pursue personally meaningful goals and make in impact on their social context. (Sykes, 2016, p. 82)

Overall, it is clear that although previously learner autonomy had been considered in the domain of education, it moved more specifically into the domain of language education during the twenty first century.

Notice that in all these examples, all three pieces of information are present: the author's/organization's name, the date of publication (or n.d. if the date is unavailable) and the page number where the information came from (or paragraph number if the material is not paginated). When using in-text citation for quotation, all three aspects are required.

Paraphrasing

Paraphrasing information means giving the same information as in the original text, but in different words. Most source material that is mentioned in one's writing is paraphrased. It is preferred that writers use paraphrasing rather than quotation because the reader wants to know what the writer thinks. The writer takes the idea from the source material but writes it in their own words in their writing. In this way, they can emphasize the parts that they feel are important. Although the words and emphasis are their own, the idea has come from a source material they read. Therefore, in-text citation is required. Paraphrasing is more difficult than quotation, because the words cannot be taken directly from the source material; rather, the writer needs to change the words substantially, without changing the meaning.

Keck (2006) created a taxonomy of paraphrase types that was created to evaluate student paraphrasing. This taxonomy demonstrates what we mean by "substantial revision." In general, this means that every word should be paraphrased except for particular terms or phrases that are unique to that topic or discipline. Every other word should be paraphrased—not only the words, but also the sentence structure should be substantially changed.

Take a look at the following two examples:

Original:

I am determined to make Japan a country where opportunities for women abound, and glass ceilings are a thing of the past. Already, the number of working women has grown by 800,000 over the past 2 years, exceeding 27 million as of January.... To keep more Japanese women in the workforce, we need to provide them more support outside the workplace. This is why I expanded the number of openings at child-care facilities by 200,000 since 2013 and increased assistance for families raising children. Last year, a new parental leave system went into effect, making it easier for both mothers and fathers to take time with their families.

Writing with in-text citation:

Prime minister Shinzo Abe, in his commentary to the *Japan Times* (2015), insisted that his social policy reforms designed to allow women to fulfill their potential as contributors to Japan's economic growth had caused the working women population to grow to its present point, exceeding 27 million—a rise in 800,000 workers over the past 2 years.

Original:

The tangible results of these developments are to be found in the rising tide of violence inflicted on refugees and asylum seekers—incidents which are reported in the headlines of the very same newspapers that have whipped up such xenophobic sentiments: "Thugs attack asylum seeker." "Refugee hurt in city gang attack." "Afghan man beaten to death after night out." "Refugee fled Saddam's torture, only to be attacked by racists."

Writing with in-text citation:

Although "refugee" has a clear legal definition, it has been found lacking as many of today's situations of forced displacement are more complex than this definition allows. For instance, many people have had to move from

their homes due to environmental disasters, state failure and socio-eco-
nomic marginalization of ethnic groups (Betts & Kaytaz, 2009, p. 26).

Notice that rather than just the name of the author or organization, an
extended introduction is used here. This is done for people who hold
important positions that make them an authority on the subject, usually
presidents, prime ministers or departmental ministers. If the author you
are citing does not have this kind of important position, then only use the
family name in the in-text citation, as in the example that follows.

Original:

Meanwhile, the international federation of the Red Cross and Red Crescent
Societies (IFRC) has made reference to people moving as a result of severe
economic and social distress. The combination of livelihood collapse, environmental disaster and state failure is increasingly contributing to nonrefu-
gees leaving their country of origin because of an existential threat for
which they have no domestic remedy.

Writing with in-text citation:

This negative labeling has discredited refugees in their efforts to be inte-
grated into a host society. Due to this labeling, these displaced people may
encounter hostilities as unjustified entrants (Crisp, 2003).

INTRODUCING QUOTED AND PARAPHRASED INFORMATION

Basically, there are two ways to introduce information which has been
quoted or paraphrased from another source. The first is to introduce the
citation information using a signal phrase that includes the name of the
author or organization. The second is to add the citation at the end of the
sentence, in parentheses.

Signal Phrases

Signal phrases can be used for both quotations and paraphrased information and are chosen when the name of the author or organization is
important. See the following examples, both of which have the signal
phrase in bold:

Quotation with a signal phrase:

Ting-Toomey (1985) **stated that** "intercultural misunderstanding and
potential conflict arise when two individuals, coming from two distinctive

cultures, have two different ways of expressing and interpreting the same symbolic action" (p. 72).

Paraphrase with signal phrase:

Van Hear (1998) **and Richmond** (1994) **have argued that** the term allows analysis of the interaction of structural factors and degrees of individual choice to explain displacement.

Note that only the family name is used. The person is introduced in the text (for example stating their position) only if this information is important (usually for presidents or prime ministers of countries, religious leaders, among others).

The choice of verb to use in a signal phrase is an important consideration. In the examples above, the verbs "stated" and "argued" have been used. However, different verbs indicate a different relationship between the writer and the source material. Table 4.1 gives examples of verbs used to indicate a positive relationship between the writer and the source material (i.e., the writer agrees with the idea of the source material), a neutral relationship between the writer and the source material (i.e., the author indicates neither agreement nor disagreement with the idea in the source material but merely lets the reader know the idea from the source material), or a negative relationship between the writer and the source material (i.e., the writer is sceptical of the idea in the source material or disagrees with it).

Table 4.1. Examples of Verbs Used to Show the Relationship Between the Writer and Source Material

Positive	Neutral		Negative
• Demonstrate	• State	• Report	• Claim
• Show	• Argue	• Explain	• Contend
• Confirm	• Indicate	• Note	• Maintain
• Point out	• Emphasize	• Describe	• Insist
• Agree	• Believe	• Define	• Assert
• Illustrate	• Suggest		• Declare

The simplest form of signal phrase is "According to." This is a neutral signal phrase that is used to introduce another writer's idea. See the following example:

Paraphrase using "according to":

According to the OECD (2015), 72% of women are employed on a full-time basis with 31% at senior management level.

Parenthetical In-Text Citation

Parenthetical in-text citation is the more common of the two methods and is used when it is the idea, rather than the author, that is of primary importance. It is used for both paraphrased and quoted material and is the preferred method. When citing more than one material at the same time, a semicolon is used to separate the information of two in-text citations. See the following examples:

Quotation with parenthetical in-text citation:

From a purely psychological perspective, learner autonomy is "the capacity to take control of one's own learning" (Benson, 2011, p. 58).

Paraphrasing with parenthetical in-text citation:

Team teaching in the field of English language education in Japan has become a broadly familiar educational innovation in recent decades, largely through the establishment of the JET programme in 1987, which places non-Japanese Assistant Language Teachers in school classrooms with Japanese Teachers of English for team teaching purposes (Brumby & Wada, 1990; Miyazato, 2006).

These previous in-text citation examples include citation for two different source materials, both of which include the same idea. The first material was written by two authors: Brumby and Wada, while the second material was written by Miyazato. Notice the semicolon between the two in-text citations as well as the use of ampersand (&) between the names of the two authors of the first material. In APA style, ampersand is always used in parenthetical in-text citations, whereas the word "and" is used in signal phrases.

Citing Information That Has Been Cited by Others

Students are not the only ones who use in-text citation. Most of the academic source materials you read will cite source materials that they have read. Therefore, sometimes when reading academic source materials about your topic, you will come across in-text citations for other materials. If the information that has been cited from another source is relevant to your writing, rather than citing the information directly, you should use the information in the reference section of the material to find the original material and read it. If the information is used in your writing, you would then use the citation and reference information for the original material, not the material which cited the original.

This is done for two reasons. It is important not to take information out of context. It is also possible that the author of the citation may have made a mistake in the information they have provided, thus constituting plagiarism. If you copy material which has been quoted by someone else into your own writing as a quotation, and even if you paraphrase the information into your own words, without checking the information in the original material, you will also be guilty of plagiarism if such a mistake is present. Even if such a mistake is not present, when paraphrasing information which has been cited by someone else, it is extremely difficult not to take the information out of context without having read the original to understand the intention of the idea.

The only exceptions to this rule are when the original material is not available in a language that you can understand and when the original material is no longer available (such as very old materials which are out of print or historical documents). In these exceptional cases when we cite information which was cited in another material, we need to write information for both materials in the in-text citation. This takes the form *Name (Year, as cited in Name, Year)* in a signal phrase and *(Name, Year, as cited in Name, Year)* in a parenthetical in-text citation. The former information citing the original material, while the latter information cites the material which the writer read. See the following example:

Citation of a citation using a signal phrase:

In terms of the quality of the feedback itself, Nakanishi and Akahori (2005, as cited in Hirose, 2008) compared high level Japanese students' point-scale evaluations of their peers' writing as well as descriptive feedback.

In this example, Hirose (2008) included a citation of Nakanishi and Akahori (2005). The writer of the above sentence read the material by Hirose (2008) only, not the material by Nakanishi and Akahori (2005).

Citation of a citation using parenthetical citation:

It has been stated that less direct feedback methods are superior to more direct methods because of the additional cognitive processing involved (Lyster, 2002, as cited in Sheen, 2004).

In this example, Sheen (2004) included a citation for Lyster (2002). The writer of the sentence read the material by Sheen (2004) only, not the material by Lyster (2002).

Note that only the materials actually read by the writer (Hirose, 2008; Sheen, 2004) appear in the reference list. No material which was not read by the writer should ever be included in the reference list, although credit is given to the original author of the idea in the in-text citation as seen in the previous examples.

REFERENCES

Abe, S. (2015, April 27). Opinion: When women can thrive, so will Japan and the world. *The Japan Times.* Retrieved from http://www.japantimes.co.jp/opinion/ 2015/04/27/commentary/japan-commentary/when-women-can-thrive-so-will-japan-and-the-world/#.WHLPZmPOaIU

Benson, P. (2011). *Teaching and researching autonomy* (2nd ed.). Harlow, England: Pearson Education.

Betts, A., & Kaytaz, E. (2009). *National and international responses to the Zimbabwean exodus* (New Issues in Refugee Research, UNHCR Working Paper no. 175). Retrieved from http://www.unhcr.org

Brumby, S., & Wada, M. (1990). *Team teaching.* London, England: Longman.

Crisp, J. (2003). *A new asylum paradigm? Globalization, migration and the uncertain future of the international refugee regime* (Working paper no. 100). Geneva, Switzerland: United Nations Higher Commission for Refugees. Retrieved from http://www.unhcr.org/cgi-bin/texis/vtx/home/opendocPDFViewer .html?docid=3fe16d835&query=%22New%20issues%20in% 20Refugee%20Research%22

Dillard, C. (1994). Beyond supply and demand: Critical pedagogy, ethnicity, and empowerment in recruiting teachers of color. *Journal of Teacher Education, 45*(1), 9–17.

Hirose, K. (2008). Peer feedback in L2 English writing instruction. In K. Bradford-Watts, T. Muller, & M. Swanson (Eds.), *JALT2007 Conference proceedings* (pp. 543–552). Tokyo, Japan: JALT.

Keck, C. (2006). The use of paraphrase in summary writing: A comparison of L1 and L2 writers. *Journal of Second Language Writing, 15,* 261–278.

Miyazato, K. (2006). *Role and power sharing between native and non-native EFL teachers: Three cases of teach teaching in Japanese high schools* (Unpublished doctoral dissertation). Temple University, Philadelphia.

OECD Sweden. (2015). *Closing the gender gap.* Retrieved from http://oecd.org/ gender/closingthegap.htm

Richmond, A. H. (1994). *Global apartheid: Refugees, racism, and the new world order.* Oxford, England: Oxford University Press.

Sheen, Y. (2004). Corrective feedback and learner uptake in communicative classrooms across instructional settings. *Language Teaching Research, 8*(3), 263–300.

Sykes, J. (2016). Learner autonomy. In C. Williams, R. Ruegg, N. Araki, M. F. Agnello, P. C. Miller, & L. DeWitt (Eds.). *Readings for academic writing* (pp. 79–83). Akita, Japan: Akita International University Press.

Ting-Toomey, S. (1985). Toward a theory of conflict and culture. In W. B. Gundykunst, L. P. Stewart, & S. Ting-Toomey (Eds.), *Communication, culture and organizational processes* (pp. 71–86). Beverly Hills, CA: SAGE.

Van Hear, N. (1998). *New diasporas: The mass exodus, dispersal and regrouping of migrant communities.* London, England: UCL Press.

Yamagata Prefectural Museum. (n.d.). Welcome to Yamagata Prefectural Museum! Retrieved from http://english.yamagata-museum.jp/

Zapata, J. (1988). Early identification and recruitment of Hispanic teacher candidates. *Journal of Teacher Education, 39*(1), 19–23.

5

MAKING YOUR REFERENCE LIST

WHY DO I NEED A REFERENCE LIST?

Including a reference list is necessary for two primary reasons. First, it tells the reader that you have done your research as the writer on the topic you have chosen. This makes you more credible on the topic. Second, a reference list gives readers enough information to help them find any of your sources that they might be interested in reading on their own. Without this information, it might be very difficult for the reader to find your sources.

WHAT SHOULD I INCLUDE IN MY REFERENCE LIST?

Everything you cite in the text should be included in the reference list. Likewise, everything in your reference list should be cited in the text. If you did not cite the material in your text, then you should not include it in your reference list. At the same time, as noted in Chapters 2 and 4, it is important to avoid plagiarism. With that in mind, every source you consult and from which you take information and include in your own writing must be cited in the text and included in the reference list.

WHERE DOES THE REFERENCE LIST GO IN MY ESSAY?

Your reference list goes at the end of your essay. Typically, the reference list should start on a new page, not on the last page where your conclusion ends. However, you may wish to ask your instructor where she or he

The Concise APA Handbook
pp. 39–49
Copyright © 2017 by Information Age Publishing
All rights of reproduction in any form reserved.

prefers the references to start. In order to help conserve paper and save the environment, some instructors may tell you it is okay to simply start your reference list after the conclusion.

HOW SHOULD I FORMAT MY REFERENCE LIST?

There are several key points in formatting your reference list:

1. Your reference list should start with the word "References" (without quotation marks) centered at the top of the page. This word should *not* be underlined, bolded, or written with capital letters. It should look *exactly* like this:

References

2. References should be listed in alphabetical order by whatever appears first in each entry.
3. Your references should be formatted the same as the rest of your paper with 1-inch margins.
4. Your references should be double spaced all the way through. This means that each line of each entry should be double spaced, not just between entries.
5. Although APA does not have a specific required font, fonts that are difficult to read should be avoided. APA and most instructors recommend using 12-point Times New Roman.
6. Your references should be formatted with a hanging indentation set to 0.5 inches (see Chapter 6 to learn how to set a hanging indentation).

HOW SHOULD I FORMAT EACH REFERENCE?

There are several basic rules to follow in order to format each reference. It is important to understand that each type of reference does have slightly different requirements. Below are examples of the most common types of references, but first, let's look at the basic rules that apply to most references.

There is some important basic information you should look for in your sources that you will need to include in each reference. This information must be provided in a particular order, but sometimes this information is not relevant to some types of references. There are other sources that might also require different or additional information, such as music, film, and television. However, most sources used in academic papers will typically follow this order:

1. Author(s) name(s) in the order they appear in the source [See the note below]
2. Publication date
3. Title of the source
4. Title of the book/journal/website the source comes from
5. Volume and issue number (usually only journals, magazines & newspapers)
6. Page numbers (except for some online sources)
7. DOI number for an academic journal source
8. URL for a website source

NOTE: Western sources typically print names in the order of first (given) name, middle name (if there is one), then family name at the end. On occasion, Western sources do print them with family name first. You can tell that the family name is listed first, because there will be a comma separating the family name from the first name. If there is no comma, it is in order of first name and family name. Also note that many sources published in Asia print names in the opposite order: family name first, then first (given) name. Regardless of the order in which they appear in the source, in your reference list, you must always list them with the family first, and then given name initials.

(Examples follow on the next page.)

EXAMPLES

Academic Journal Articles

One author with CrossRef DOI:

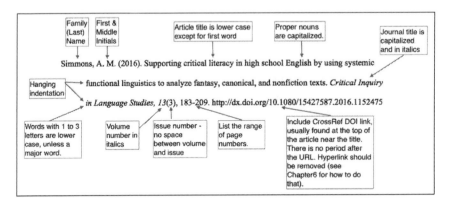

One author with old style DOI:

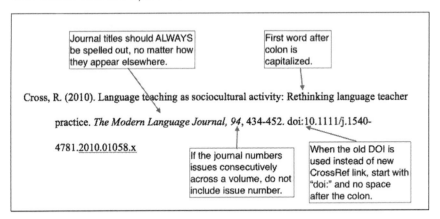

Two to seven authors:

With two or more authors, all authors should be listed in the order in which they appear in the source, last name first.

Zittoun, T., & Cerchia, F. (2013). Imagination as expansion of experience. *Integrative*

Psychological and Behavioral Science, 47, 305-324. doi:10.1007/s12124-013-9234-2

A comma should separate EVERY author.

More than seven authors:

List the first 6 authors and the last author only. They should be listed in the order in which they appear in the original source.

DeSmet, A., Van Ryckeghem, D., Compernolle, S., Baranowski, T., Thompson, D., Crombez, G., ... De Bourdeaudhuij, I. (2014). A meta-analysis of serious digital games for healthy lifestyle promotion. *Preventative Medicine, 69,* 95-107. doi:10.1016/j.ypmed.2014.08.026

Use an ellipsis (3 periods) between the 6th and last author to replace any additional authors.

An online journal article:

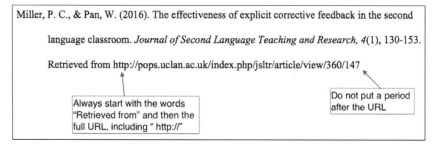

Miller, P. C., & Pan, W. (2016). The effectiveness of explicit corrective feedback in the second

language classroom. *Journal of Second Language Teaching and Research, 4*(1), 130-153.

Retrieved from http://pops.uclan.ac.uk/index.php/jsltr/article/view/360/147

Always start with the words "Retrieved from" and then the full URL, including " http://"

Do not put a period after the URL

An article in a language other than English:

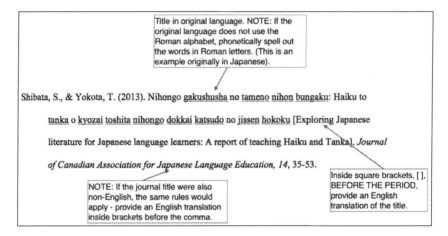

Books

An authored book:

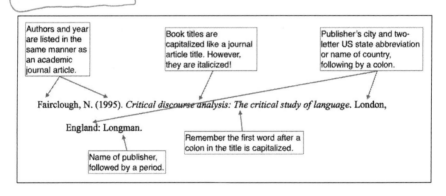

An edited book (whole book):

The only difference with an edited book and an authored book is that you must put "(Eds.)." after the last editor's name, but before the year of publication.

Elliott, C., Stead, V., Mavin, S., & Williams, J. (Eds.). (2016). *Gender, media, and organization:*

Challenging mis(s)representations of women leaders and managers. Charlotte, NC:

Information Age.

If the publisher is in the US or Canada, you should put the two-letter state or province abbreviation after the city instead of the country name.

A digital book for a specific electronic device:

Carlson, D. (2012). *Leaving safe harbors: Toward a new progressivism in American education*

and public life [Kindle version]. New York, NY: Routledge. Retrieved from

Amazon.com

Digital books require the format to be included inside brackets before the period. The first word is capitalized, and following words are lower case.

Include the basic URL for this type of digital source.

An online book:

Clough, G. W. (2013). *Best of both worlds: Museums, libraries, and archives in a digital age.*

Washington, DC: Smithsonian Institution. Retrieved from

http://www.si.edu/content/gwc/BestofBothWorldsSmithsonian.pdf

If the book is online, include the URL with the words "Retrieved from" before the URL.

A book in a language other than English:

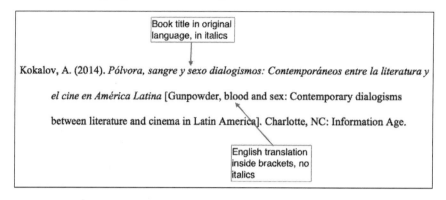

Book Chapters

A chapter in an edited book with different editor(s) and author(s):

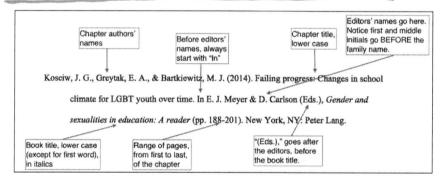

A chapter in a book with an author, no editor:

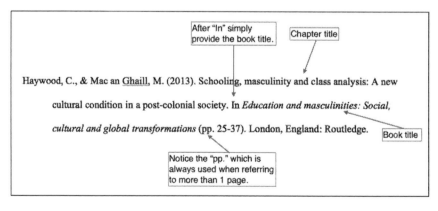

Miscellaneous Online Sources

Youtube video—user's real name known:

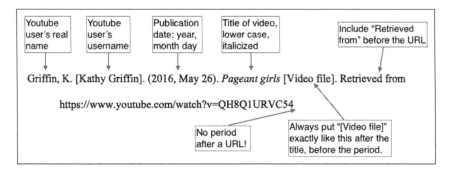

Youtube video—only user's username known:

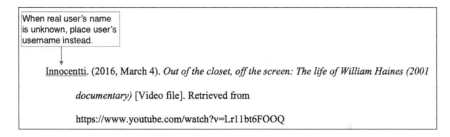

Online data report:

NOTE: In many cases, an online data set or report will be formatted like an online book.

Kosciw, J. G., Greytak, E. A., Palmer, N. A., & Boesen, M. J. (2014). *The 2013 national school climate survey: The experiences of lesbian, gay, bisexual and transgender youth in our nation's schools.* New York, NY: GLSEN. Retrieved from http://www.glsen.org/nscs

Online data set from a government agency:

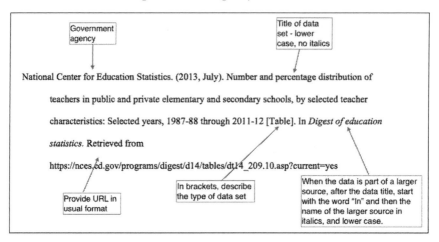

Online newspaper:

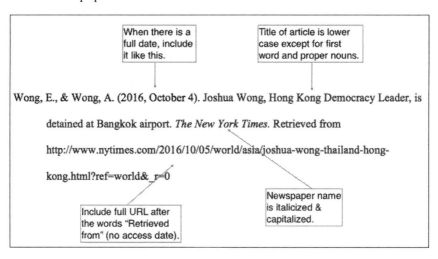

Online newspaper, no author:

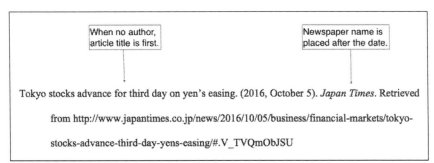

Tokyo stocks advance for third day on yen's easing. (2016, October 5). *Japan Times*. Retrieved

from http://www.japantimes.co.jp/news/2016/10/05/business/financial-markets/tokyo-

stocks-advance-third-day-yens-easing/#.V_TVQmObJSU

Miscellaneous Other Sources

Source with no publication date:

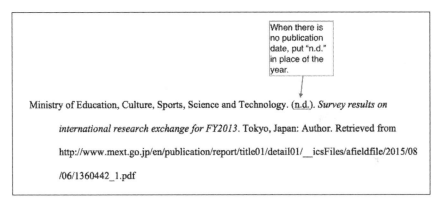

Ministry of Education, Culture, Sports, Science and Technology. (n.d.). *Survey results on*

international research exchange for FY2013. Tokyo, Japan: Author. Retrieved from

http://www.mext.go.jp/en/publication/report/title01/detail01/__icsFiles/afieldfile/2015/08

/06/1360442_1.pdf

Document where author and publisher are the same:

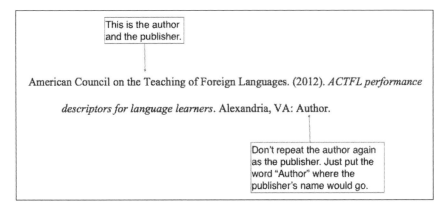

American Council on the Teaching of Foreign Languages. (2012). *ACTFL performance*

descriptors for language learners. Alexandria, VA: Author.

6

FORMATTING

Proper formatting is an integral part of making your article look professional while abiding by the standards that APA sets. In this chapter we will outline some of the key areas of formatting and guide you through the process of implementing them. This is intended to be a very general outline of formatting, to assist you with the basics.

In this section we will look at the following formatting rules:

- Font and font size
- Line spacing
- Running head
- Margins
- Section titles
- Heading titles
- Bullet and lists
- Page breaks
- Putting diagrams, pictures, or graphs inline
- Indenting text such as long quotes

FONT AND FONT SIZE

The recommended font used for APA is Times New Roman and the recommended size is 12. To choose this, click "Home" in the menu bar. The

The Concise APA Handbook
pp. 51–69
Copyright © 2017 by Information Age Publishing
All rights of reproduction in any form reserved.

"Home" menu items will appear and will look something like what is seen in Figure 6.1.[1]

Figure 6.1.   Example of a home menu bar.

Choose Times New Roman and 12 pt. size (Figure 6.2).

Figure 6.2.   Where to choose the font and appropriate size.

This is decided because the font is easy to read and that size is ideal for the reader.

LINE SPACING

All lines of your text should be double-spaced, including the text, references, tables, and appendices. This rule has been set because it also allows the editor and reader to easily determine the article length.

Under the "Home" menu, find the icon that looks like Figure 6.3:

Figure 6.3.   Example button to change line spacing.

When you click on it, you will be given a number of line options. Choose 2.0, as indicated in Figure 6.4.

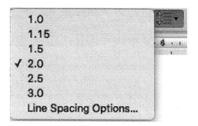

Figure 6.4.   Example of line space drop box menu.

If you have already typed some text, you can highlight that text and then set the spacing.

MARGINS

The next items that need setting are the margins. Margins are the top, bottom, right and left side "borders" of your paper that can be thought of like a frame around the text. This will be mentioned in the next section, but the top margin will contain your running head and your page numbers. This is separate from your text and they do not interfere with each other. To set your margins, choose "Layout" from the menu tabs, as seen in Figure 6.5.

Figure 6.5.   Sample "layout" button.

Depending on your version of Word, this might look slightly different, but the most important item to realize is that you need to set your margins to "1 inch" or "2.54 cm," depending on whether your working from Imperial Units or Metric.

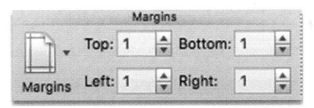

Figure 6.6.   Margins setting in inches.

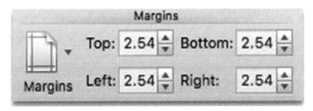

Figure 6.7.   Margins setting in centimeters.

Figure 6.6 shows the margins in inches, while Figure 6.7 shows them in centimeters.

RUNNING HEAD

Now that you have set your margins, one of the items that goes in the top margin area or "header" is called the "running head." It is the title or a shortened title of your paper and starts on the very first page of your paper, the title page. This is the part of your paper that tells the reader the title of your paper at the top of each page.

The most important point to remember is that the running head on the first page of your paper will be different than the running head on the rest of the pages in your paper. Normally, putting in a header is very easy, but because the first page is different, you need to change a setting in Word. To begin, let's put in the header the easy way, then change the settings.

To put in a header, double click with your mouse at the very top of any page (in the top margin area) in your document to activate the header, as shown in Figure 6.8.

Figure 6.8.   Activating the header.

You will know the header is activated when the top margin looks like the following image:

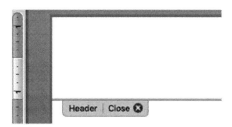

Figure 6.9.   Example of an activated header area.

The formatting of the running head is the same as the rest of your paper, Times New Roman and 12pt font. At the start of the left margin in header, type the following:

Running head: TITLE OF YOUR PAPER OR MAX 50 CHARACTERS

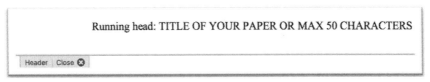

Figure 6.10.   Example of a running header in the header.

It should look like the example in Figure 6.10. "TITLE OF YOUR PAPER OR MAX 50 CHARACTERS" should be your own title or a shortened version of it, since the running head (your title part) should be **no more than 50 characters including spaces**. Also it should be in all capital letters.

If you highlight your title part, you can check the "Characters (with spaces)" and make sure it is 50 or less. In Figure 6.11 it is 40 characters in length.

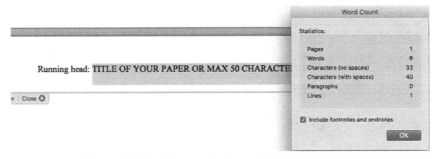

Figure 6.11.   How to check word/character count.

If you close the header (click on "Close"), you'll see your running head become lighter than the other text in your paper. This is normal. This helps differentiate your running head text with the text in your paper.

Now, if you scroll through your document, you will see the running head appear at the top of all pages. What we want to do next is to make the first page different from the rest of your pages in your paper. The first page tells the reader "Running head:" so that the reader knows that this is the running head. On the second, third, fourth, and following, pages of your paper, you do not need the words "Running head," you just need the actual running head only.

Go to the second page of your paper and double click with your mouse in the header area.

A menu item will appear next to "Home." It is the Header and Footer options menu similar to Figure 6.12. Click on it.

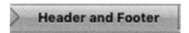

Figure 6.12.   Example of a header and footer button.

Depending on the version of Word or whether you operate Windows or Mac, you will notice an option called "Different First Page." This needs to be checked as seen in Figures 6.13 and 6.14.

Figure 6.13.   Mac version of the Options menu for changing the header and footer.

Figure 6.14.   Windows version of the Options menu for changing the header and footer.

Notice that the "Different First Page" button has been clicked, so now all you need to do is go to the top of the second page and delete the text "Running head:." Highlight the text "Running head:" and push the delete button (see Figure 6.15).

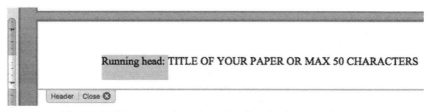

Figure 6.15.   Removing "Running head:" from 2nd page.

It should now look like this (Figure 6.16):

TITLE OF YOUR PAPER OR MAX 50 CHARACTERS
Header
Close

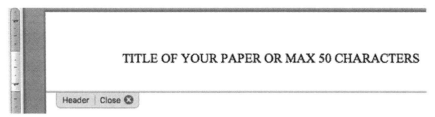

Figure 6.16. "Running head:" removed from header on 2nd page and beyond.

Click on the "Close" button to close your header. If you scroll to the top of your paper, to the very first page, you will see the running head as shown in Figure 6.17:

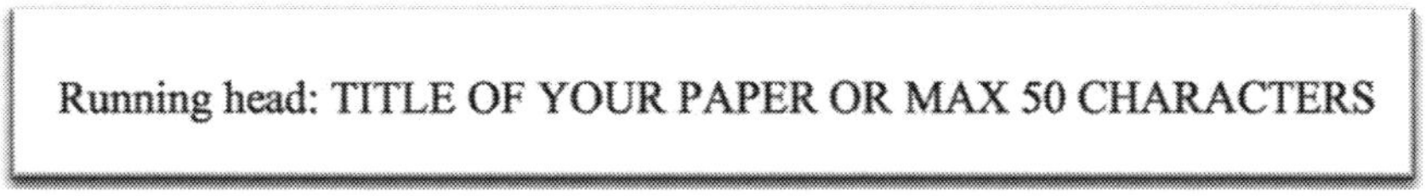
Running head: TITLE OF YOUR PAPER OR MAX 50 CHARACTERS

Figure 6.17. How the title page (first page) of the paper should look.

If you scroll through the rest of your document, you'll see the other pages like the image in Figure 6.18:

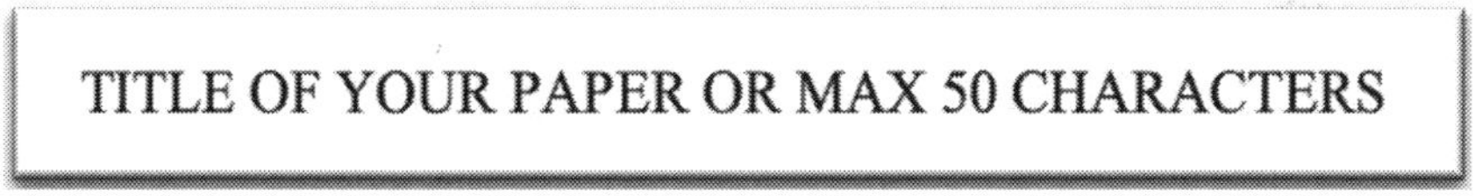
TITLE OF YOUR PAPER OR MAX 50 CHARACTERS

Figure 6.18. How pages 2 to the end of the document should look.

Now you have set your "Running Head."

SECTION TITLES AND HEADING TITLES

The next part of your formatting that you need to pay attention to will be the section and heading titles within your paper. Each section or each part of your paper requires a heading, and the level of the heading requires a different type of formatting.

Before we start, here are a few formatting icons that you need to know. They are located in the "Home" menu of Word.

B

This is the **Bold** icon on the home menu. You highlight the text and click on the Bold icon to make the text Bold, or click on the Bold icon to make the text normal again. You can also use Ctrl+B on the keyboard as a shortcut (Command+B on a Mac).

I

This is the *Italics* icon on the home menu. You highlight the text and click on the Italics icon to make the text italicized, or click on the Italics icon to make the text normal again. You can also use Ctrl+I on the keyboard as a shortcut (Command+I on a Mac).

This is the centering icon. Highlight the text you want to center and push this icon.

This is the left justify icon. Usually text is left justified as a default, but if you need to change the justify to left, highlight the text and click this icon.

SECTION TITLES

For the *section titles* of your paper, you will need to use regular font formatting (no boldface, no italics). These include following:

Title of Your Paper

Author Note

Abstract

References

Footnotes

Appendix/Appendixes

Each of these section titles should be capitalized (as you see in the list above), and your title should have all major words capitalized. These are the titles that make up the general structure of your paper.

The title of your paper should be on the title page as well as on the first page where your text begins. Section titles should be centered and on their own line. A section also generally begins on a new page. (The only exception is for the author note section, which goes on the title page.)

HEADING TITLES

For your heading titles, you should use boldface formatting. The heading titles are different than the section titles, these heading titles are for introducing different parts of your paper. This is sometimes referred to as "signposting," or in other words, telling the reader what is coming in the next text. These occur in the paper specifically between the "Abstract" and "References" sections.

Table 6.1 is a simple chart to help you with the formatting rules for headings.

Level	Format
Table 6.1.	How to Format Headings Based on Level
1	**Centered, Boldface, Uppercase and Lowercase Heading** Below you should start your paragraph, and should be indented.
2	**Flush Left, Boldface, Uppercase, and Lowercase Heading** Below you should start your paragraph, and should be indented.
3*	**Indented, boldface, lowercase paragraph heading ending with a period.** Your paragraph begins right away, in the same line as the heading.
4*	***Indented, boldface, italicized, lowercase paragraph heading ending with a period.*** Your paragraph begins right away, in the same line as the heading.
5*	*Indented, italicized, lowercase paragraph heading ending with a period.* Your paragraph begins right away, in the same line as the heading.

Note: * in headings 3, 4, and 5 be careful! The very first letter of the heading is capitalized and all the rest of the letters are lowercase. Of course, if a heading contains a colon, then the word following the colon should be capitalized. Also, if there are proper nouns they too should be capitalized.

Your paper will have these headings, but do not number the headings (The numbering here is only to illustrate the level of heading). A Level 1 heading is used for the largest sections of your paper, such as the beginning of the introduction, literature review, methodology, and so forth. A Level 2 heading is used for the next largest sections that are inside of a Level 1 heading. They are used to break up the larger Level 1 headings into smaller, easier-to-understand sections. Many shorter papers will only need Level 1 and possibly Level 2 headings. Larger research papers may also wish to break up Level 2 sections into smaller chunks with Level 3 headings, and so forth. The idea is that you should always start with Level 1 headings to start the largest sections of your paper, and then progress to Levels 2 through 5 as necessary to divide your paper into smaller sections.

BULLETS AND LISTS

The next items to cover are the bullet lists. If you need to create a bullet list, then there are a few simple rules you need to follow.

Figure 6.19. Sample "bullet" button.

Figure 6.19 is the icon that you use when you want to make a bullet list. You can do this two ways, first by making the list, then highlighting it and then clicking on the bullet list icon, or you can click on the icon, and start making your list. For the next bullet to appear, you need to push the "enter" or "return" key on your keyboard. For a bullet list to appear, you need a hard return at the end of each item on the list.

Here is an example of a bulleted list.

- You put one item here.
- You put the next item here.
- You put one more item here.

At the end of the list, just click on the bullet list icon to turn off the bullet function. In the list above, each of the items begins with a capital letter and ends with a period.

If you need to make a bullet list to emphasize a number of elements in a sentence, then you need to follow the capitalization and punctuation as if it were a sentence. If you wanted to make a bulleted list midsentence, then

- you should start with the first important item;
- then put the next item; and
- finally end with the last item as if this entire list was a sentence.

INSERTING A PAGE BREAK

Rather than pressing the "Enter" key repeatedly to move down to a new page, it is preferable to simply insert a "page break" between the end of the text on the current page and where you wish to begin the new text. A new page should be started using this feature to start the first page of main text (after the title page), the beginning of the references list, and at the beginning of each appendix. The following image (Figure 6.20) shows you where you may find this function.

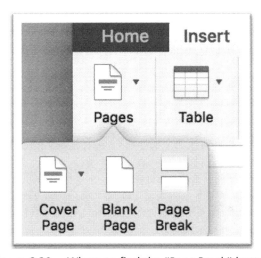

Figure 6.20. Where to find the "Page Break" button.

As an example, when you add an appendix to your paper, you will need to make sure that the references and each appendix begin on their own new page. The appendix always occurs after the reference section. What you'll need to do is place your cursor by clicking at the end of the conclusion or references section. You might need to hit the "Enter" or "Return" key a few times. Then click on the Insert menu, choose Pages, then choose "Page Break." This will automatically put your cursor at the top of the next page. Then you can start your references section or appendix section. When you change your essay, even if the length of the text on the pages prior change, the page break feature ensures that the text after the page break occurs on the following page.

Using the editing marks to show you, the following is an example of before and after applying a page break after the references section, creating an appendix on a new page.

Figure 6.21. The "editing marks" button.

Figure 6.21 is the editing marks button (if you click on this you can see various formatting marks). You can find this button in the Home menu.

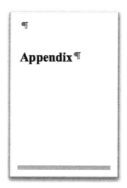

Figure 6.22. Sample of what a page with the editing marks revealed.

The word "Appendix" has been typed a few lines down from the last reference. The bottom of the page Figure 6.22 shows there is no new page at this point, but after we apply a page break, this is what we see in Figure 6.23.

Figure 6.23. Sample of a page with a "Page Break" inserted.

There is a "Page Break" indication (if you want to check this, click on the editing marks button in the "Home" toolbar. Notice that the "Page Break" is followed by a new page and the title "Appendix" begins on a new page, as it should.

PUTTING DIAGRAMS, TABLES, AND GRAPHS INLINE

When you put something other than text into the body of your paper, there are a few options to choose from to make sure that your diagram, picture, or table moves with the rest of the text. Sometimes a picture can be a floating picture, meaning that as you add text before or after the diagram, the diagram does not move "with the text." Here is an example using a simple object to represent a diagram, picture, or graph has been added to the document (Figure 6.24).

Figure 6.24.   Sample "picture."

If we click on that object, then in the menu bar, we would see "Format" or "~~~ Format." What we want to find is the "Wrap Text" icon, which can be found directly under the "Format" menu item, as shown in Figure 6.25:

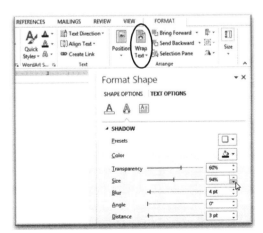

Figure 6.25.   Where to find the
"Wrap Text" option in the image "Format" menu.

Or it can be found under "Arrange" as shown in Figure 6.26.

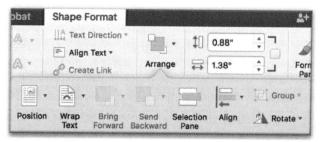

Figure 6.26.   Finding the "Wrap Text" feature through the "Arrange" button.

The "Wrap Text" icon looks a little different depending on your version of Word. If you click on it, you will be given a menu of choices of how the diagram, picture, or graph will move with the text, or how it will sit on the page. "In Line with Text" (see Figure 6.27) ensures that the object stays with the text and moves with the text, even if you were to add or remove text above the object. Your object in this case can be treated like a big text letter; in other words, if you put your cursor before it and press enter, it will respond like a word, and move to the next line. You can even choose to center it on the page using the "centering" icon in the "Home" menu.

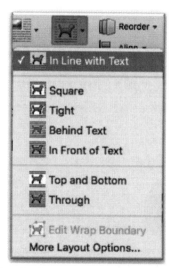

Figure 6.27.   Setting image to be in line with the text.

If you were to choose "Through," then the object just sits on the page and the text moves underneath it as shown in Figure 6.28.

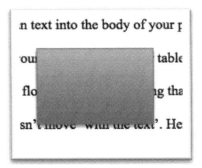

Figure 6.28.   Example of image set to "through" text.

If you chose "Square," your text would move around the object. Figure 6.29 is an example where the diagram sits on the page and the text moves "around it."

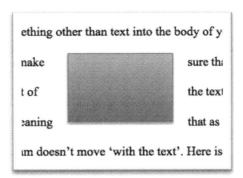

Figure 6.29.   Example of an image set to "square."

For academic writing, the most appropriate would be "In Line with Text."

INDENTS

The last item that will be discussed will be the indents. The two icons for this can be found in the Home menu. They look like those in Figure 6.30.

Figure 6.30. Sample "indent" buttons.

If I need to indent text, such as a long quotation (see Chapter 4), I would highlight the text and then click on the "Increase indent" button (the one with the arrow pointing to the right), so I can imagine pushing the text to the right. The text should be indented about 2.54 cm or 1 inch. Below, in the example, a long quote (more than 40 words), is indented. Note, too, there are no quotation marks used in a long quote and the final punctuation mark follows the text, not the closed parentheses.

> Here is an example of a long quote. Here is an example of a long quote. Here is an example of a long quote. Here is an example of a long quote. Here is an example of a long quote. Here is an example of a long quote. (Author, 2016, p. xx)

After the long quote, you would hit the enter or return key and then click on the "Decrease indent" button, to return the cursor to the left margin. The formatting of the text (double spaced and left justified) remains unchanged in the long quote.

Finally, there is another type of indentation that is necessary for any paper that uses references and is formatted according to APA guidelines. This is called a "hanging indentation." Your references should be formatted with the first line of each reference starting at the beginning of the left margin. The following lines of **the same reference** should be indented 0.5 inches (1.27 cm). Your references will look like the examples in Chapter 5.

In order to set the hanging indentation, it is important that you ONLY use the "Return" or "Enter" key at the end of each reference. Allow each reference to automatically wrap to the next line. If you do not follow this step, your hanging indentations will not set properly. Make sure your line spacing is set to double spaced (see Figures 6.3 and 6.4 in this chapter). After you have typed the word "References" at the center of your page, press the "Return" or "Enter" key once before typing your first reference into the list.

Next, under the "Format" menu, choose "Paragraph" (see Figure 6.31).

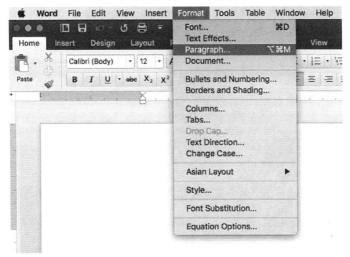

Figure 6.31.   Accessing the menu for formatting the paragraph.

Once you have opened the paragraph menu, you will see a window similar to that found in Figure 6.32.

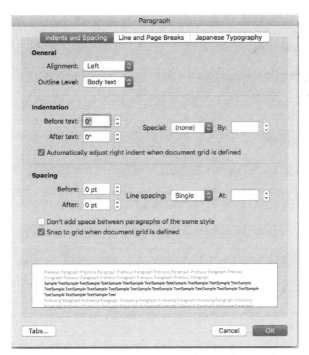

Figure 6.32.   Sample paragraph formatting options.

Next, about one third of the way down the window is the "Special" and "By" options. Click on the dropdown menu for "Special" and choose "Hanging." And next to the "By" option, click on the up arrow until it reads "0.5" or you can manually type that in. When you are finished click on "OK" at the bottom of the window. See Figure 6.33 for an illustration.

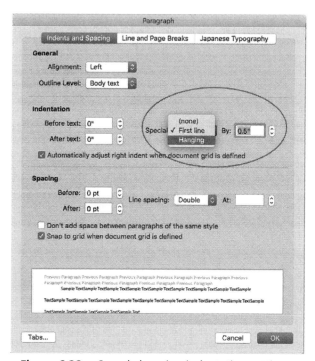

Figure 6.33. Sample hanging indentation settings.

If you have already typed your references, you can achieve the same formatting by simply highlighting all of your references, and going through these same steps. When you are finished, your references should look something what is shown in Figure 6.34.

References

Claycomb, C., & Hawley, W. D. (2000). *Recruiting and retaining effective teachers for urban schools: Developing a strategic plan for action.* College Park, MD: University of Maryland. (ERIC Document Reproduction Service No. ED451 147)

Dillard, C. (1994). Beyond supply and demand: Critical pedagogy, ethnicity, and empowerment in recruiting teachers of color. *Journal of Teacher Education, 45*(1), 9-17.

Gay, G. (2002). Preparing for culturally responsive teaching. *Journal of Teacher Education, 53*(2), 106-116.

Goodwin, A. L. (1997). Historical and contemporary perspectives on multicultural teacher education. In J. King, E. Hollins, & W. Hayman (Eds.), *Preparing teachers for cultural diversity* (pp. 5-22). New York: Teachers College Press.

Figure 6.34.   Sample of references with hanging indentation.

NOTE

1.   All figure images are used with permission from Microsoft.

49159774R00045

Made in the USA
Middletown, DE
09 October 2017